"Having the author take me through ....
honour... especially as I was not judged by her:
nothing I said that would have been a shock did not
shock the author, again I could open up even more to
her and go into personal details."
-Chelsea (Client)

"This book is really well illustrated and very well
thought out. It really opened my mind to things I
hadn't thought of before. It's very well written.
Highly recommended! This book left me feeling
really uplifted and found it very helpful. loved it!"
-Abi (Customer)

"The workbook gives a strong pathway through
understanding and applying the principles of CBT in
a Christ-centered way. I highly recommend this
workbook for small groups in churches or treatment
programs."
-Suzanne (Executive director at Foundation House
Ministries)

"For wanting her readers to experience an
improvement in their mental state of mind with the
intervention of the Great Physician, I'm giving Ms.
Roskilly 5 STARS"
-Robin Morgan (Book Reviewer)

Acknowledgements

To my kids- Thank you for helping when my health is bad, you are amazing, kind, loving, caring, considerate and strong young people and I'm so proud of you and the young people you are and have become.

To my friends and family- you have supported me through the dark times and stuck with me and held me up, emotionally and physically!

Thank you to those who have been supportive and instrumental in helping me with this book. Be it through prayer, advice, reviewing, and help with editing.

I'm not including names for privacy reasons. You all know who you are.

Thank you!

Table of Contents

Prologue

My Testimony

Throughout my life I have suffered from depression and anxiety. Some of this was circumstantial and some was down to my own lack of resilience.

It first began when I was a teenager. I moved to a new school at fifteen, into year ten - the beginning of GCSE's. It was tough as I had no friends and the new school was more academic than the previous one. I soon found out I wasn't up to the standard I should have been at that time. We'd just moved house again too and I felt really alone. However, there was one girl who let me sit with her on the first day and we were instantly friends. As the term went on, I made a few other friends and it became more bearable. Then, it began, I started fainting; I would just blackout, sometimes two to four times a week or two or more times a day, but despite tests, doctors couldn't work out what was going on.

To try to help, my mum taught me to meditate and one day she took me to a spiritualist church, she also did tarot card readings with me. One day we were in one of the shops in the Brighton lanes, I remember seeing a purple velvet spell book, which I was instantly attracted to. Mum bought it for me. In my bed-room, I set up a blanket on my chest of drawers, lit candles and incense and tried out the spells in the book. At the time, I loved it. It was something I was in control of.

Back at school, apart from the first friend I met, the rest of the girls soon got fed up of me fainting. Whether that was the reason, or something else, to this day, I don't know, but suddenly they turned against me, they would call me names across the classroom or snigger at me in the hallways. This made me very upset and self- conscious, along with my physical health and the exams piling up I began to feel really low. During the holidays I thought I would try a specific spell, to get the girls to stop. When I returned to school, after a week I realised I hadn't had any more trouble from them, I was amazed, really pleased with "my powers" and most certainly relieved! I scraped through my exams and came out with five GCSE's. This then led to me doing what I wanted; Performing Arts at college in 2000. These turned out to be some of the best years of my life.

I made some new friends, was dancing, performing on stage and ultimately, doing what I loved and the fainting seemed to ease. It was also where I met my partner. I was hoping to go to RADA or some other swanky performing arts in higher education, as my dream, was to become an actress. When I finished at college, we decided to audition at Butlins to be redcoats. Though we were both doing well and going through all the stages, just as we were about to get our places, they found out we were a couple and their rules were not to take on any couples or allow redcoats as couples. Then in the final round, my partner did that bit better than me and they took him on. So, to stay together I went in as catering staff, which was a bit of a blow to my self- esteem!

As the months went on. I felt more and more alone, as there was no one I really connected with, it wasn't the life I was hoping for and never saw my partner either as he was partying every night, I would join in occasionally but really it became a bit much. One night I walked into a room where they were doing the Ouija board, I was interested and stayed to watch.

Trigger warning**

Then one day, I found out something that made me feel very hurt, unloved and extremely alone. It was this, along with everything else I was feeling, that led me to do what I did next.

I went for a walk round the town, in a daze, I bought two packets of paracetamol from every chemist I could, went to a bathroom and I took the lot. Then as I wandered back to my room to bed, still feeling completely numb, it was then I saw the person who hurt me who apologised profusely and said they still cared. I told them what I'd done, and got whisked to the nearest hospital, where I was made to drink charcoal, to induce vomiting and was kept in over-night. I never returned to the camp and my mum picked me up.

Because of low self- esteem I went back to my partner. The following year, we were in a pub and an older gentleman approached our table, he was telling me things about myself he shouldn't have known, he then began talking about witchcraft, he had his own coven and asked me to join, I was excited and took his number. That night without my knowledge, my partner called our window cleaner, a Christian, (though my partner wasn't a Christian himself at the time). That night we spoke for ages, or at least he spoke, I was quite defensive and pretty irritated by him! But in the middle of a video on creation, it felt like I had a light bulb turn on inside me and I knew that I was sinful and that Jesus had died for me and I needed to repent and turn to him! I said the sinner's prayer, with the guidance of the window cleaner, and immediately knew I had to get rid of my rune stones and spell books. After he'd left, I stayed awake until 3am, filled with the Holy Spirit and writing my first Christian poem (seen in the next section).

The following thirteen years were bittersweet. It was a continuous rollercoaster, of mostly lows, but included, marriage, homelessness (adultery, addict-ion and arrests - though these weren't on my part, I hasten to add!) and other things, but the highs were my two beautiful children, who gave me a reason to keep going.

I worked in care homes as a carer, activity coordinator, catering supervisor and in recent times took on a university degree, BA Hons in Health and Social Care, with the Open University. I soon gained some confidence and courage to apply for divorce.

In 2016 I began working for a local Christian charity, where we took services into care homes, I coordinated 52 teams in the local vicinity, organised events and led services and prayer meetings. I absolutely loved it!

The fainting had been on and off over the years, undergoing test after test at the hospital. But now cardiology was on the case as well. The stages in between bouts of fainting didn't give quite enough time for me to take driving lessons (as I had to be faint free for two years before getting into a car) but in 2018

I got my provisional licence, took lessons, passed my test and bought my first car just before Christmas. Everything was finally falling into place, the kids were happier, I was enjoying my job and now I was finally driving.

My walk with God over the years just became better and better, He was my friend, my guide, my companion as well as my saviour. In the darker times he was my comforter and in the good times he was there with me.

I was studying mental health as part of the degree and during my prayers one day God put on my heart that I should raise awareness of mental health within the church and to write about how to help those in faith in improving their health and wellbeing. Over the next year and a half, I began making notes as and when He prompted me.

Then in March 2019, the fainting started again. I was driving home one day and I came over feeling spaced out and dizzy. I pulled up by the side of the road, ate a packet of crisps, sunk a bottle of water then made it home. As I was coming up the stairs to the flat with the shopping a neighbour stopped to chat and before I could do anything about it, I was unconscious on the floor. However, every time I tried getting up, I kept blacking out, an ambulance was called and I was taken to hospital, I spent almost a week on the cardiology ward. I was due to take my first ever solo church service at a local church that Sunday, about which I was so excited and felt so blessed about doing. Instead, I spent it in the hospital. After being discharged I spent the next year fainting so regularly, I had to go on sick leave from work and was told by doctors and the DVLA not to drive. I had yet more tests done and, in July 2018, finally, the cardiologist gave me a diagnosis, Neurocardiogenic Syncope (which is to do with low blood pressure, having a bradycardic and occasionally irregular, heart rate and the signals from there to the brain being very slow). But the words he said to me are what really stuck, "There is no cure or treatment for it". My heart sank, and I cried, a lot. This began the start of the depression again and soon I was on antidepressants and was referred for counselling and CBT.

I was stuck indoors, not being able to get out because of the syncope. My daughter was helping me whenever I had episodes and was doing the cooking and cleaning. It was a dark time and I began self – harming. Looking back, I realised it was something I could be in control of, as everything else was totally out of my control. It was horrid. I couldn't do anything to stop the fainting, I couldn't do things a mum should be able to do, I missed driving them to school, parents' evenings, I hated it. Everything was out of my control and self- harming was the only thing that gave that control back to me. However, I was ashamed of it and hid it from everyone. I withdrew from family and friends, I wanted to be on my own and yet I felt so alone. I began keeping a diary. Here is just one entry from around that time;

"Ok, so I am on quite a few support groups...be good if there was one for all; Psoriasis, Neurocardiogenic Syncope, depression, anxiety and self - harm... oh, and loneliness... just about had enough... if it wasn't for the kids, I would end it all now, hate feeling like this... life sucks! I mean what's the point? Try to find distractions and hobbies, but what does that actually do... absolutely

nothing, there's no end to it all, can't I just end it?? Apparently not! Y? Because I know my kids need me and apparently Jesus loves me, aaargh!! Why is this so hard?? And yes, it's been four weeks but I finally gave in, I cut again... and you know what? I don't even care!"

The thing was, I did care, I cared a lot and that was the trouble. Days turned into weeks and weeks to months, eventually I became fed up of feeling the way I was. I wasn't feeling particularly close to Jesus at the time, but started talking to Him again just small prayers like, "Help me Lord, I'm fed up of feeling like this." Within a few weeks I began listening to some worship music again. Then another week or two later, a book from my large Christian collection, which I hadn't touched for ages, caught my eye. It was called "Toxic Emotions" by Mary Alice Isleib. Wow, what an eye opener! It spoke of how I was feeling, as though it was written for me! She is a Christian writer who made me realise that I didn't have to feel bad about how I was feeling but also helped me to acknowledge and recognise what I was feeling, eliminate shame and improved my relationship with God, Wow! As the weeks went on, I carried on listening to worship music, prayed more and more and ploughed through the book. She explained that in order to receive healing we needed to break through denial, as David (in the bible) did.

I had finally reached the point that I wanted. I was ready to accept my pain and difficulties and wanted release from it. At this realisation I literally cried out to God, bawling my eyes out, I was asking Him to release me and relieve me from the darkness.

Over the next week, I began to reach out to my family

and a few close friends from church. I admit-ted the self- harming to one friend and asked for prayer. There were a lot of tears, it was hard enough to admit that I had a problem myself but saying it out loud was another thing! However, she was supportive and prayerful. As the next few weeks went on, I continued with the prayer, worship music and reading.

The kids and I were due to go away with a friend a month later. The fainting had got so bad, I rang her and said I didn't want to be a burden and to cancel. She wasn't having any of it and insisted on picking us up so that I could relax in the caravan insisting I wouldn't be a problem. Bless her!

The day before we were due to drive up to the site she asked if we wanted to go along to the church they go to the following morning before we left. I felt ready to go to church again, so I agreed.

We sat in the congregation, I worshipped along with everyone else and listened to the sermon. Then at the end they asked if anyone wanted to go forward for prayer, whilst the tea and biscuits were being served. I looked at my friend and she at me. I said "Do we have time?" to which she smiled at me and replied "definitely." The lady asked what I wanted prayer for and I said just for the Neurocardiogenic syncope. As they prayed, I followed along and agreed in my heart. Then I felt I was going to fall, without a moment's notice I was on the floor, but it wasn't the usual, I wasn't unconscious, it was the Holy Spirit. I heard the lady going on to pray for any negative emotions I was experiencing; I hadn't mentioned anything like that to her! When they'd finished, I felt such a sense of relief, peace and freedom, I just knew I was healed!

In the following weeks and months, I realised the Neurocardiogenic Syncope hadn't been healed but the toxic emotions definitely had! No more, did I feel that despair, lack of control or the darkness that I previously had. Thank you, Lord! Since then, I've had circumstances, including long and nasty Neuro-cardiogenic Syncope episodes, where I couldn't even sit upright without blacking out and was stuck in bed and had migraines for 10 days. This would have usually sent me to that mindset of despair, but the Lord has kept me strong and in His peace. I'm not saying I'm perfect, I'm not, but I am a very long way off from where I was, mentally, emotionally and spiritually and that is down to God and certain people in my life (you know who you are!). It was also due to gaining a certain amount of resilience, self- esteem and confidence, which I developed through all of this as well as the CBT and counselling sessions I attended.

Lauren Roskilly

Poem- Night of Conversion

Silence is broken with just one word,

Like an invasion on life.

There was never any care, but still it was heard.

Is there no such thing as a choice in life?

No sign until now.

Then a torture of words telling me to sacrifice.

Is there never any justice in this place?

Are we all trapped?

Then comes along the one we should know and eventually
have to face.

The sense of freedom is like an open window,

The beginning of a new path.

Ditch the devil and then with our love, we must go.

Search your heart and you will find,

The route of fate.

Then set out and let your journey unwind.

Synopsis

What's the purpose of writing the book?

As you have already read, in the Prologue, I've experienced poor mental health throughout my life. But most importantly, God has put on my heart to share with you how He helped me through those storms and dark times, in order to help and encourage others. I have also been researching and asking individuals on many different Christian mental health groups across social media platforms to provide me with short testimonies as to how God has helped them in their journeys, specifically those who have experienced mental health issues, particularly anxiety and depression. These can be found after the sessions. These, too, may offer encouragement and hope.

What does the book consist of?

Ideas, scriptures, formulas and CBT related questions and techniques to help improve mental health and wellbeing. In addition to this 'Testimonies', which are stories of how God has helped others in improving their mental and emotional health and well- being.

Self- help? Isn't that contradicting the Christian faith?

I've called it "self- help" because that is the classification this book comes under. But our help should really come from the Lord. This book does both. We need to knock at the/His door and He will gladly open it for us. The Lord can help guide us through our journey of improving our mental health. Each session, includes prayer; offering our whole selves to Him, scripture and meditation.

<u>Are you qualified to write such a book?</u>

I suppose I'm a lay person, with first- hand experience. Relevant qualifications are:

- Honours Degree in Health and Social care, modules included;

  'Leadership and Management in Health and
      Social care'
  'Mental Health and community'
  'Approaches to Mental Health'
  'Adult, Health, Social care and wellbeing'
  'Perspectives in Health and Social Care'
  'An introduction to Health and Social care'

- Diploma in Psychology and CBT

- Certified shorter courses including:

      'Exploring the relationship between
      anxiety and depression', Level 3
      'Mindfulness in mental health and
      prison settings', Level 2
      'Understanding depression and
      anxiety', Level 2

What is Mental Health?

Approximately 25% of British adults will experience a mental health problem in any one year so it isn't (or shouldn't be) something to hide, be ashamed of or not talk about. Just as you might go to the doctor for physical symptoms, your mind is also important and there are plenty of resources available, including your G.P, that can help to improve your mental health and well - being.

> "Mental health is defined as a state of well-being in which every individual realizes his or her own potential, can cope with the normal stresses of life, can work productively and fruitfully, and is able to make a contribution to her or his community." *(WHO, 2020)*

Put simply, mental health is about our emotional and psychological wellbeing. Though, it is also down to resilience, how we react to situations and the control we have over our responses.

Our responses are the ways in which we think, behaviours and actions.

This is summarised in four parts.

1/ Being aware of the surroundings, physical and socially and how we interact with these.

2/ The ability to make choices and set goals according to our capacity to do so.

3/ Being able to relate to others appropriately and enjoy relationships.

4/ The ability to respond emotionally to both positive and negative situations and be able to return to a less emotional state.

Having all these abilities in place can mean you are in a state of good mental health and can reduce the chance of the following factors, effects and symptoms from occurring.

Physical factors or ways in which our bodies react to stress (physiological reactivity) include; raised blood pressure and heart rate, digestion stopping or slowing and sweating can increase, plus many others.

With these factors, long-term effects can occur. These include; inducing anxiety, depression, sleeping problems, loss of appetite, low self-esteem, constant worry, dizziness, headaches, irritability and increased use of alcohol or drugs, along with other effects.

From viewing these, it is understandable how a vicious circle can occur.

Circumstances & situations> stress, worry & sadness> factors & symptoms> circumstances & situations.

As just seen, prolonged stress can be detrimental to our physical and mental health. But it can be the way we react and respond to these stressors that is the key and we all deal with life's storms differently.

Professionally, there are many ways in which mental health can be approached and dealt with and in the majority of cases the individual and/or their general practitioner (G.P) can decide which route they want to go down. These are briefly explained next, followed by how we can apply and incorporate some of these concepts and treatments with biblical reasoning, understanding and encouragement.

Mental health can also be due to chemical imbalances in the brain, which can bring on symptoms of bipolar, schizophrenia and others. These symptoms may be hard, almost impossible for the individual experiencing them to recognise. It usually takes someone close to the individual to recognise these in order to get the correct help and diagnosis.

Psychiatric and Biomedical Approaches

This approach is about medical treatments, for instance medicine, to control or reduce the above symptoms and any additional physical symptoms. However, these approaches also include the offering of advice to cope with any related stresses, in order to avoid future relapses.

This approach normally follows on from a process of diagnosis and is generally the main basis of inter-vention for many who have been diagnosed with mental health problems.

This is generally centralised on scientific knowledge and evidence-based medicine (EBM), which is where service users are involved in their research. This approach can be seen as being scientific. It is this approach that deals with the more severe mental health cases, for instance psychosis. If you feel you are experiencing any of the following symptoms, please see your doctor.

These are:

- Hallucinations- Seeing, hearing, smelling,

tasting or feeling things that don't exist in reality.

- Delusions- Beliefs that are in fact untrue.

- Confused and disturbed thoughts- rapid and disturbed speech and loss in train of thought.

(NHS 2019)

Psychological Approaches

This approach is very broad but can be narrowed down to being the scientific study of the human brain and the influences that lead to how an individual thinks, feels and acts. A psychologist works to explain the current and changing behaviours of individuals or groups.

There is a wide variety of specialities nowadays. For instance; practitioners, counsellors, therapists and psychologists. These are all available online or via your general practitioner and accessible to anyone requiring them.

There are plenty of branches of psychology that are available, but the five most predominant ones are: social, cognitive, educational, biological and developmental psychology.

Social Approaches

Social psychology is the branch that looks at how an individual interacts within their social environment or society. It works with the notion that depression is linked to life events and whether or not an individual is receiving any social support to help deal with these.

As in psychology, this approach seeks to understand how an individual behaves in terms of their thoughts, actions and feelings in relation to society or group settings.

The treatment is an alternative approach, from the ones above. As it mainly comes from service user activists or "survivors", also known as lay people and also those from the social work field. But peer support and the development of self-management strategies are also frequently used. Along with support from specific centres and groups. For instance, community support groups.

Cognitive Approaches

These approaches are predominately to do with the mind. Including; thought processes, perceptions, beliefs etc.

This approach began in 1969 by Ulrich Neisser, following his research on perception, memory, thought patterns, problem solving and attention. He went on to write a book on 'Cognitive Psychology' *(APS, 2012)* which was the beginning of this approach.

There are many areas where cognitive approaches are used. For instance; child development, selective attention, learning styles and Cognitive Behavioural Therapy (CBT).

CBT approaches and techniques are the focus for this book.

Cognitive Behavioural Therapy (CBT)

CBT is defined as being a talking therapy which addresses and challenges an individuals' negative and distorted thoughts about themselves and the world. This is done through helping individuals to behave and think more positively, it offers guidance in how to improve and how to respond to challenges, which can help individuals to increase resilience. CBT can also help to break any vicious circles or behaviours that may cause distress. For instance, through transference, which is the redirection of feelings and emotions onto another object or person.

This is all done through models and techniques which can help to change thought processes, for instance, the way one thinks, feels and behaves. From negative distortions, beliefs and behaviours to more positive ones. It is these three elements (thoughts, feelings and behaviours) that are the focus of CBT.

CBT is a short-term psychotherapy which is used to treat behaviours including depression, anxiety, anger, phobias, conflict resolution, loneliness, substance abuse, adjustment, personality issues and even chronic pain.

CBT was first practiced by Aaron Beck, a psychoanalysis practitioner. During this practice he recognised the link between the thoughts and feelings of his clients. He soon discovered that a combination of cognitive therapy and behavioural techniques produced the best results.

At the core of CBT is the assumption that, whilst external events can cause a great deal of distress, most individuals inadvertently maintain their own suffering through irrational beliefs. That's not to say you are irrational, or your thoughts and beliefs don't matter, but what it does mean is that some of those, specifically negative ones, aren't necessarily true, despite what is believed. But CBT can help an individual to differentiate between what's irrational and what's not and help to change these thought processes.

CBT has the largest evidence base, which means that more studies are carried out on this therapy than on other talking therapies and is currently considered the gold standard talking treatment by the NHS. (*NSA, 2020*)

Lauren Roskilly

Mindfulness

You may have heard the phrase 'being mindful' before and may have noted that this, in practice, isn't something you would hear within the church.

Being 'mindful' in the secular terms is about taking time to be in the moment and recognise the present time. It can also be about the senses; what you can see, hear, smell, feel and taste.

It's being aware of these senses in addition to your own thoughts and feelings, noticing what your mind is doing and also paying attention to your body and breathing.

These aspects are to help individuals focus on the present moment, as opposed to what is going on around them. For instance, looking at what is in front of you and how you are feeling as opposed to the circumstances and situations around you.

Mindfulness in Christ

This is a concept I prefer to use; using mindfulness from a biblical perspective. Using the New International Version (NIV) throughout the book. Scripture says;

Romans 8.6 The mind governed by the flesh is death, but the mind governed by the Spirit is life and peace.

Colossians 3.2 Set your minds on things above, not on earthly things.

Matthew 22.37 Jesus replied: Love the Lord your God with all your heart and with all your soul and with all your mind.

Psalm 46.10 Be still, and know that I am God. I will be exalted among the nations; I will be exalted in the earth.

So, we can be mindful of Christ, the Father and the Spirit.

Being Mindful of the Trinity

1) Take time, in the current moment, to stop, connect and listen to the Holy Spirit.

2) Recognise how you are feeling and what your body and breathing are doing.

3) Offer all of these to God, through Jesus.

4) Submit to Him, this means to give Him ALL of you.

5) Prayerfully ask for His comfort, peace, joy and strength and anything else He wants to offer you freely, according to His plan.

Being Mindful of His Earth

1) Look at what's in front of you. What can you see, hear, smell, feel and taste that God has provided for us?

2) Offer Him thanks for these things and for anything else He has provided you with.

3) Be still. Spend some time thinking and praying about these things.

How to practice Biblical Meditation

1/ Eliminate distractions.

2/ Get comfortable.

3/ Lay your hands comfortably in front of you, open them with palms facing up; allow yourself to be open to the Holy Spirit.

4/ Start with prayer: giving thanks and asking God to join you and guide your time together.

5/ Use scriptures and verses and consciously repeat them over and over, keeping your mind focused on these and the Holy Spirit.

6/ If your mind wanders, bring it gently back to the scripture/ verse you are focusing on.

7/ Stay in this place for as long as desired. Recommended time: 5 mins - 1hr.

Scripture References

Here are references to refer to at any time. You can find each of these in the Holy Bible, New International Version.

For Sadness & Depression-

Comfort:

Job 36: 15 But those who suffer he delivers in their suffering; he speaks to them in their affliction.

Psalm 23: 4 Even though I walk through the darkest valley, I will fear no evil, for you are with me; your rod and staff, they comfort me.

Psalm 55: 22 Cast your cares on the Lord and He will sustain you He will never let the righteous be shaken.

Psalm 119: 52 I remember, LORD, your ancient laws, and I find comfort in them.

Psalm 139: 7-8 Where can I go from your Spirit? Where can I flee from your presence? If I go up to the heavens, you are there; if I make my bed in the depths, you are there.

Isaiah 66: 13 As a mother comforts her child, so will I comfort you; and you will be comforted over Jerusalem.

Jeremiah 31: 13 Then young women will dance and be glad, young men and old as well. I will turn their mourning into gladness; I will give them comfort and joy instead of sorrow.

John 14: 1-4 Do not let your hearts be troubled. You

believe in God; believe also in me. My Father's house has many rooms; if that were not so, would I have told you that I am going there to prepare a place for you? And if I go and prepare a place for you, I will come back and take you to be with me that you also may be where I am. You know the way to the place where I am going.

2 Corinthians 1: 3- 4 Praise be to the God and Father of our Lord Jesus Christ, the Father of compassion and the God of all comfort, who comforts us in all our troubles, so that we can comfort those in any trouble with the comfort we ourselves receive from God.

2 Corinthians 1: 7 And our hope for you is firm, because we know that just as you share in our sufferings, so also you share in our comfort.

Strength:

Deuteronomy 31: 6 Be strong and courageous. Do not be afraid or terrified because of them, for the LORD your God goes with you; he will never leave you nor forsake you."

1 Chronicles 16: 11 Look to the LORD and his strength; seek his face always.

1 Chronicles 29: 12 Wealth and honour come from you; you are the ruler of all things. In your hands are strength and power to exalt and give strength to all.

Psalms 28: 7 The LORD is my strength and my shield; my heart trusts in him, and he helps me. My heart leaps for joy, and with my song I praise him.

Isaiah 41: 10 So do not fear, for I am with you; do not be dismayed, for I am your God. I will strengthen you and help you; I will uphold you with my righteous right hand.

Isaiah 40: 29-31 He gives strength to the weary and increases the power of the weak. Even youths grow tired and weary, and young men stumble and fall; but those who hope in the Lord will renew their strength, they will soar on wings like eagles; they will run and not grow weary, they will walk and not be faint.

Ephesians 6: 10 Finally, be strong in the Lord and in his mighty power.

2 Corinthians 12: 9-10 But he said to me, "My grace is sufficient for you, for my power is made perfect in weakness." Therefore, I will boast all the more gladly about my weaknesses, so that Christ's power may rest on me. That is why, for Christ's sake, I delight in weaknesses, in insults, in hardships, in persecutions, in difficulties. For when I am weak, then I am strong.

Philippians 4: 13 I can do all this through him who gives me strength.

For Worry & Anxiety-

Peace:

Psalms 34: 14 Turn from evil and do good; seek peace and pursue it.

Psalms 37: 11 But the meek will inherit the land and enjoy peace and prosperity.

Isaiah 26: 3 You will keep in perfect peace those whose minds are steadfast, because they trust in you.

John 14: 27 Peace I leave with you; my peace I give you. I do not give to you as the world gives. Do not let your hearts be troubled and do not be afraid.

John 16: 33 "I have told you these things, so that in me you may have peace. In this world you will have trouble. But take heart! I have overcome the world."

Romans 15: 13 May the God of hope fill you with all joy and peace as you trust in him, so that you may overflow with hope by the power of the Holy Spirit.

Ephesians 6: 15 and with your feet fitted with the readiness that comes from the gospel of peace.

Philippians 4: 6-7 Do not be anxious about anything, but in every situation, by prayer and petition, with thanksgiving, present your requests to God. And the peace of God, which transcends all understanding, will guard your hearts and your minds in Christ Jesus.

Philippians 4: 9 Whatever you have learned or received or heard from me, or seen in me—put it into practice. And the God of peace will be with you.

2 Thessalonians 3: 16 Now may the Lord of peace himself give you peace at all times and in every way. The Lord be with all of you.

1 Peter 5: 7 Cast all your anxiety on him because he cares for you.

Reassurance in trials, storms and sickness:

Psalms 41: 3 The LORD sustains them on their sickbed and restores them from their bed of illness.

Psalms 73: 26 My flesh and my heart may fail, but God is the strength of my heart and my portion forever.

Proverbs 18: 14 The human spirit can endure in sickness, but a crushed spirit who can bear?

Isaiah 4: 6 It will be a shelter and shade from the heat of the day, and a refuge and hiding place from the storm and rain.

Isaiah 25: 4 You have been a refuge for the poor, a refuge for the needy in their distress, a shelter from the storm and a shade from the heat. For the breath of the ruthless is like a storm driving against a wall

Matthew 9: 12 On hearing this, Jesus said, "It is not the healthy who need a doctor, but the sick.

Luke 22: 28 You are those who have stood by me in my trials.

John 11: 4 When he heard this, Jesus said, "This sickness will not end in death. No, it is for God's glory so that God's Son may be glorified through it."

2 Thessalonians 1: 4 Therefore, among God's churches we boast about your perseverance and faith in all the persecutions and trials you are enduring.

1 Thessalonians 3: 3 so that no one would be unsettled by these trials. For you know quite well that we are destined for them.

James 1: 12 Blessed is the one who perseveres under trial because, having stood the test, that person will receive the crown of life that the Lord has promised to those who love him.

Changing perceptions

1 Chronicles 16: 11 Look to the LORD and his strength; seek his face always.

Matt 6: 9-13 "This, then, is how you should pray: "'Our

Father in heaven, hallowed be your name, your kingdom come, your will be done, on earth as it is in heaven. Give us today our daily bread. And forgive us our debts, as we also have forgiven our debtors. And lead us not into temptation, but deliver us from the evil one.

Luke 21: 19 Stand firm, and you will win life.

John 10: 10 The thief comes only to steal and kill and destroy; I have come that they may have life, and have it to the full.

John 14: 26 But the Advocate, the Holy Spirit, whom the Father will send in my name, will teach you all things and will remind you of everything I have said to you.

Romans 8: 6 The mind governed by the flesh is death, but the mind governed by the Spirit is life and peace.

Romans 12: 2 Do not conform to the pattern of this world, but be transformed by the renewing of your mind. Then you will be able to test and approve what God's will is—his good, pleasing and perfect will.

Ephesians 1: 13 And you also were included in Christ when you heard the message of truth, the gospel of your salvation. When you believed, you were marked in him with a seal, the promised Holy Spirit,

Ephesians 6: 10-1 Finally, be strong in the Lord and in his mighty power. Put on the full armour of God, so that you can take your stand against the devil's schemes.

James 1: 2 Consider it pure joy, my brothers and sisters, whenever you face trials of many kinds,

James 4: 7 Submit yourselves, then, to God. Resist the devil, and he will flee from you.

1 Peter 5: 9 Resist him, standing firm in the faith, because you know that the family of believers throughout the world is undergoing the same kind of sufferings.

Introducing Christian Based Cognitive Behavioural Therapy (CBCBT)

CBCBT is a concept I've been thinking about for a while. The idea; a course to help people improve their mental health and wellbeing and improving faith, by combining CBT practices with Christianity, namely, prayer and scriptures, stories, teachings etc, from the Holy Bible.

It is aimed mostly toward those dealing with anxiety and depression. Though, I would like to make it clear that this is not a cure it's more of a self- help course. Designed to help change your focus from any negative situations, thoughts, beliefs, toxic emotions and behaviours to more positive ones and towards God and His word. By doing this it will also help to build resilience and responses to circumstances, stress and trials. It's more of a process than a quick fix and will help you on your journey.

In this book the CBCBT approach is in the form of eight sessions, which I recommend to be done on a weekly basis to gain the best influence and impact on how you respond to each section. This also gives you a chance to work through each, taking on board each activity, weekly tasks and suggested scripture meditations. This can be done individually or in small groups.

CBCBT

Let's get started...

If you are doing this individually, really think about each session, being as honest with yourself as possible and ask God for guidance. Then at the sharing points, use this time for reflection, making sure you have addressed everything that's related to that session and share with God.

I, Lauren, am also a coach and offer support & accountability alongside the following 8 sessions at a fraction of the price of coaching. If you are working individually and believe this may be of use for you. Check out mindfulofchrist.net/coaching.

If you are in a small group, there isn't any pressure to share, if you are not comfortable to. It's up to each individual to feel safe and work through what's going on for them. Bear in mind that it helps to share, but only when the time feels right for each individual.

Between each session, regularly reflect back on your notes from the previous session and offer the same or similar prayers to God, adapting if needed for that particular day and how you are feeling. There's space between each session to keep a thought diary (journal), which I encourage you to do. Make notes on your thoughts, feelings, behaviours and responses to certain situations you experience. This can help you to recognise how you are at that particular time, as this isn't always obvious. This is important as it brings negative thoughts, feelings and behaviours to the surface as opposed to pushing them down and bottling them up. This is when further symptoms or behaviours can potentially develop, affecting both you and others around you.

Then have a look at the scriptures (provided at the end of each session) and meditate on each of them. Or you can find and use any scripture that God gives you. Where it states about meditation; refer to the page 29 'How to practice Biblical meditation.'

IF IN SMALL GROUPS: HAVE SOMEONE IN LEADERSHIP TO LEAD AND GUIDE THE GROUP THROUGH EACH SECTION.

Don't forget, be honest with yourself and support others when working in groups.

Session One:

Mental Health Assessment

1)Firstly, let's pray...

Dear Lord,

Thank you for being with me/us today. Please be with me/us as I/we go through this session. Guide thoughts and feelings and draw to attention anything I/we don't yet recognise, but may need addressing. Please give me/ us your strength to carry on in this day and the following week.

Thank you, Lord. Amen

2) Looking at the list on the following page, check the box next to any symptoms you may have experienced in the past two weeks. Don't forget; be honest with yourself.

Psychological symptoms:

Feelings of sadness	
A loss of interest in activities	
Low self-esteem	
Feelings of guilt	
A tendency to cry or feeling on the edge of tears	
Irritability and intolerance	
Little or no motivation	
Difficulty in making decisions	
Feelings of anxiety or worry	
Self-harm or thoughts of self-harm	
Suicide attempts or thoughts of suicide	

Physical symptoms:

Moving or speaking more slowly than usual	
Changes in weight or appetite	
Constipation	
Aches and pains that have no obvious explanation	
Low energy levels	
Loss of libido	
Changes to menstrual cycle (in women)	
Disturbed sleep (trouble staying asleep, waking up too early or sleeping too much)	

Total score: ___

(Adapted and inspired by the PHQ-9 and GAD 7 form)

If you ticked from 1 - 5: Complete the sessions in this book and follow the activities and meditations in between each.

If you scored between 5 – 10: Complete the sessions in this book and follow the activities and meditations in between each. In addition to seeking advice from someone you trust and/or your G.P.

If you scored 10+, and/or marked the last two of the psychological symptoms: Speak with your general practitioner. This may be a difficult step to make, but it is important to do so. Seeking advice from church leadership can help gain extra support too. Then complete the sessions in this book and follow the activities and meditations in between each.

3/ Answer the following questions as honestly as you can.

Do you find it hard to completely relax? If so, think about why this may be and what factors prevent you from doing so.

_____
_____
_____
_____
_____
_____
_____
_____
_____
_____

Do you assume that your worry and anxiety is for a good reason? If so, can you explain why this is and define the reality of these worries? Try imagining what you would say to a friend if they were in your situation.

_____
_____
_____
_____
_____
_____
_____
_____
_____
_____
_____
_____

Do you believe that other people don't experience the same problems and you feel alone?

Is this, in fact, reality?

_____
_____
_____
_____
_____
_____
_____
_____
_____
_____
_____

DID YOU KNOW?
1 in 4 people experience mental health issues at sometime within their lives.
(The Open University, 2015)

Think about anything that's positive in your life and the world around you.

_____
_____
_____
_____
_____
_____
_____
_____
_____
_____
_____
_____

4/ If you are working individually look back through what you have written and write down, what you would like to change and/or stop doing. In addition to this think about realistic ways in which you may be able to make these changes.

E.g., Stopping a negative habit, learn how to relax more, improve your self - esteem or be able to make decisions.

If you are working as a group, try and encourage each other to share, but you only need to share what you are comfortable with. You might be surprised at how others are feeling and possibly experience similar thoughts. It's important to note that trust is earned and confidentiality within your small group is of utmost importance.

Make notes below.

_____
_____
_____
_____
_____
_____
_____
_____
_____
_____
_____
_____

5/ Again pray...

- ♦ Offer everything from the session to God.
- ♦ Ask for His help in your progress in improving your mental health and wellbeing.
- ♦ Give thanks for all the positive things in your life.

This week:

→ Keep offering your worries and concerns to Him each day

→ Think of things that make you happy, and do them!

→ Keep a diary, note down your feelings, behaviours and any events or situations that trigger these. You can use the 'Thought Diary' space below.

→ Practice biblical meditation, using the following scriptures and any that God puts on your heart.

<u>**Meditation**</u>

Follow the guide on page 29 'How to practice Biblical Meditation'.

Suggested scriptures:

Romans 8. 10 What we suffer now is nothing compared to the glory He will reveal to us later.

1 Peter 5. 7 Casting all your anxieties on Him because He cares for you.

Hebrews 13.5 I will never leave you or forsake you.

Thought Diary

Session Two:

Stress and Responses

1) Firstly, let's pray...

Dear Lord,

Thank you for being with me/us today. Please be with me/us as I/we go through this session. Guide thoughts and feelings and draw to attention anything I/we don't yet recognise, but may need addressing. Please give me/us your strength to carry on in this day and the following week.

Thank you, Lord. Amen

2) Think about this last week.

How have you got on with the activities last week? Note: Did you do anything that makes you happy? If you have or have not done anything different, say how and why. How did this make you feel? Any improvements?

_____
_____
_____
_____
_____
_____
_____
_____
_____

_____
_____
_____

3) Think about the last few weeks...

Have you encountered any difficulties, stress or problems?

_____
_____
_____
_____
_____
_____
_____
_____
_____
_____
_____
_____

How or why did they develop?

_____
_____
_____
_____
_____
_____
_____
_____
_____

_____
_____

How have they made you feel?

_____
_____
_____
_____
_____
_____
_____
_____
_____
_____
_____

Do these experiences or feelings trigger (lead to) any specific thoughts, responses or behaviours, you have never done before, or other behaviours that you have already but have increased?

E.g., food, caffeine, drugs, alcohol, shopping, self-harm, etc.

_____
_____
_____
_____
_____
_____
_____
_____

_____
_____
_____

Do these behaviours and responses induce any further emotional and physical effects? What are they?

_____
_____
_____
_____
_____
_____
_____
_____
_____
_____
_____
_____

How do you deal with these responses?

_____
_____
_____
_____
_____
_____
_____
_____
_____
_____
_____
_____

Is there anything you would like to change, regarding your emotional responses and behaviours? If so, why?

_____
_____
_____
_____
_____
_____
_____
_____
_____
_____
_____
_____

Now, make a note on ways in which you might be able to make any changes to these behaviours. Can you replace negative thoughts, responses or behaviours with something positive?

E.g., Activities that will improve your well- being; taking a prayer, exercising, meditation, music.

_____
_____
_____
_____
_____
_____
_____
_____
_____
_____

_____

_____

4) If you are working on your own. Read back through your notes and analyse what you have written, pay attention to your responses and concentrate on the positives and any changes you are wanting to make.

If you are in a group, discuss these, share and encourage each other.

5) Again, Pray...

- ♦ Offer your responses (feelings, thoughts and behaviours) to God.
- ♦ Ask Him to be with you and guide you through the (e)motions as they come.
- ♦ Ask Him to strengthen and fill you with His peace and for His healing upon you.

Did you know?
Practicing homework can help to restructure beliefs and increase confidence.
Without this homework, skills and techniques can be overrun by negative conditioning.
(NSA, 2020)

This week:

→ Purposefully replace negative responses (thoughts and behaviours) with positive thoughts and activities,

→ Keep a diary, note down, feelings, behaviours and any events or situations that trigger these.

→ Practice biblical meditation, using the following scriptures and any that God puts on your heart.

Meditation

Follow the guide on page 29 'How to practice Biblical Meditation'.

Suggested scriptures:

Matt 11.28 "Come to me, all you who are weary and burdened, and I will give you rest. Take my yoke upon you and learn from me, for I am gentle and humble in heart, and you will find rest for your souls. For my yoke is easy and my burden is light."

John 14.27 Peace I leave with you; my peace I give you. I do not give to you as the world gives. Do not let your hearts be troubled and do not be afraid.

1 Peter 5.7 Cast all your anxiety on him because he cares for you

Thought Diary

Session Three:

Relationship and Behaviour

1) Firstly, let's pray...

Dear Lord,

Thank you for being with me/us today. Please be with me/us as I/we go through this session. Guide thoughts and feelings and draw to attention anything I/we don't yet recognise, but may need addressing. Please give me/ us your strength to carry on in this day and the following week.

Thank you, Lord. Amen

2) Think about this last week.

How have you got on with making changes?

Note: Did you manage to replace negative behaviours with positive actions or activities? If you have or have not done anything different, say how and why. How did this make you feel? Any improvements?

_____
_____
_____
_____
_____
_____
_____
_____

_____
_____
_____
_____

3) Does your mood/ behaviour have an effect or impact on your relationships?

E.g., At home, work or social

_____
_____
_____
_____
_____
_____
_____
_____
_____
_____
_____
_____

Why do you think this is?

_____
_____
_____
_____
_____
_____
_____
_____
_____

_____
_____
_____

Have people close to you said anything to you about your mood or behaviour?

If so, how did you respond? Is there anything you could have done differently?

_____
_____
_____
_____
_____
_____
_____
_____
_____
_____
_____

Is there anything that others do that you dislike and want them to stop or change?

_____
_____
_____
_____
_____
_____
_____

_____
_____
_____
_____

Have you verbalised this to the individual(s) concerned? Is so, what happened? If not, make notes on what to say to the said individual. (Focus on fact. Be specific. Note the action/ behaviour and not the individual person.)

_____
_____
_____
_____
_____
_____
_____
_____
_____
_____
_____
_____

"God never gave us the power or right to control how others respond to our "no" some will welcome it, some will hate it... Confronting an irresponsible person is not painful to him, only consequences are."

(Cloud and Townsend, 2011)

Have you forgiven them? Or anyone else? If no, then

talk to God and/ or someone you trust about how to move forward in forgiveness and prepare your heart to do so.

_____
_____
_____
_____
_____
_____
_____
_____
_____
_____
_____
_____

Think of and note down all positive relationships you may have had in the past and now.

_____
_____
_____
_____
_____
_____
_____
_____
_____
_____
_____
_____

Did you know?
The emotional support provided by social ties enhances psychological wellbeing, which, in turn, may reduce the risk of unhealthy behaviours and poor physical health.
(Umberson and Montez, 2011)

---

4) If you are working individually; Read back through these and analyse what you have written, take in your responses and concentrate on the positives.

If you are in a group, discuss these, share and encourage each other.

5) Again, Pray...

- ◆ Offer all of your feelings, behaviours and relationships to God.
- ◆ Ask Him to bring to mind anyone in need of forgiveness in your life.
- ◆ Ask Him to help you with any changes that need to be made in your life and relationships.

This week:

- → Keep referring back to what you want to change, including behaviour and forgiveness and put these into practice.

- → Keep a diary, note down your feelings, behaviours and any relationships that trigger these. You can use the space below.

- → Practice biblical meditation, using the

following scriptures and any that God puts on your heart.

<u>Meditation</u>

Follow the guide on page 29 'How to practice Biblical Meditation'.

Suggested scriptures:

Colossians 3.13 Bear with each other and forgive one another if any of you has a grievance against someone. Forgive as the Lord forgave you.

James 5.16 Therefore confess your sins to each other and pray for each other so that you may be healed. The prayer of a righteous person is powerful and effective.

Matthew 6.33 But seek first his kingdom and his righteousness, and all these things will be given to you as well.

Thought Diary

Session Four:
Making Changes and Goals

1) Firstly, let's pray...

Dear Lord,

Thank you for being with me/us today. Please be with me/us as I/we go through this session. Guide thoughts and feelings and draw to attention anything I/we don't yet recognise, but may need addressing. Please give me/ us your strength to carry on in this day and the following week.

Thank you, Lord. Amen

2) Think about this last week.

How have you got on with making changes?

Note: Did you implement positive modifiers- things that improve your mood? If you have or have not done anything different, say how and why. How did this make you feel? Any improvements?

_____
_____
_____
_____
_____
_____
_____
_____
_____

_____
_____
_____

3) Now think about your life as a whole.

On a scale of 1- 10, how content do you feel? Why?

_____
_____
_____
_____
_____
_____
_____
_____
_____
_____
_____
_____

What is your attitude on change? Do you want to change any particular aspects of life (your own and around you)? Why, or why not?

_____
_____
_____
_____
_____
_____
_____
_____
_____

> **Did you know?**
> Setting goals and reaching them is very beneficial to your mental health.
> *(SMHC, 2019)*

Do you regularly set yourself goals for any area of your life (work, relationships, health)?

If so, what are these? If not, then spend some time thinking what areas you might want to improve and what you would like to achieve, do or aim for in your life.

Use the PAPAS ART criteria:

(Adapted & inspired by the known SMART goals. Combining the SMART criteria with bible based practices.)

Pray: For God's will within your life/ To guide your steps/ Whether He wants you to "be" (with Him) or "do" (His will) at this time/ Ask him about particular situations & decisions. Then listen for His response.

Align: Do your ideas/ plans/ goals align with God's word? If you don't know, research in the Holy Bible. Speak to church elders/ leaders.

Peace: Do you experience the peace of the Holy Spirit around your ideas/ plans/ goals?

Assessable: How can you track your progress? How many? How often?
Specific: Narrow down using the five "W" questions;
>   What do you want to achieve?
>   Why do you want to achieve it?
>   Where is it located?
>   Who is/could be involved?
>   Which resources can be used or which
limitations might occur?

Attainable: Your goals need to be realistic but also should stretch your in your capabilities
Relevant: Are they relevant to the current season (day/ week/month). Is it worth your time? Are you the right person for the task/ idea/ plan/ goal?
Timely: Have a deadline, without a deadline people are less likely to complete their goals.
>   What are your goals for the year/ month/
>   week/ day? In that order! By breaking them
>   down you will see a map of how you can
>   achieve your long-term goals.

_____

_____

_____

_____

_____

_____

_____

_____

_____

Does anything happen that prevents you from achieving goals or aims in life?

E.g., Your own behaviours, attitude, health issues or outside factors.

_____
_____
_____
_____
_____
_____
_____
_____
_____
_____
_____
_____

Now think about any achievable goals for the week ahead. Break down any problems you are experiencing and write down any smaller goals that would be useful in aiming towards bigger goals and the results you are after.

Write these below and refer back to them over the week.

_____
_____
_____
_____
_____
_____

_____
_____
_____
_____
_____
_____

4) If you are working individually; Read back through these and analyse what you have written, take in your responses and concentrate on the positives.

If you are in a group, discuss these, share and encourage each other.

5) Again, Pray...

- Offer God all your responses.
- Ask for Him to bring to mind anything else that might be useful, on the subject of change.
- Ask Him for his guidance in making these changes, according to His will.
- Ask Him to give you the strength, courage and confidence you need to achieve these.

This week:

→ Keep referring back to what you want to change and the goals you have written down and put these into practice. If you don't feel like doing these, do them anyway and "act" as though you are enjoying them. When this is done regularly, it can improve motivation. If you repeat something often enough it can potentially develop into a habit and become part of your routine.

→ Keep a diary, note down, feelings, behaviours and any goals you are aiming towards and steps you take to achieve these. You can use the space below.

→ Practice biblical meditation, using the following scriptures and any that God puts on your heart

---

Meditation

Follow the guide on page 29 'How to practice Biblical Meditation'.

Suggested scriptures:

Philippians 3. 14 I press toward the goal for the prize of the upward call of God in Christ Jesus.

Eccles 3. 12 I know that nothing is better for them than to rejoice, and do good in their lives.

Matthew 6. 33 But seek first the kingdom of God and His righteousness, and all these things shall be added to you.

Thought Diary

_____

_____

_____

_____

_____

_____

_____

_____

_____

_____

_____

_____

_____

_____

_____

_____

_____

_____

_____

_____

_____

_____

_____

_____

_____

_____

_____

_____

_____

_____

_____

_____

_____

_____

_____

_____

_____

Session Five:
Frustration and Anger

1) Firstly, let's pray...

Dear Lord,

Thank you for being with me/us today. Please be with me/us as I/we go through this session. Guide thoughts and feelings and draw to attention anything I/we don't yet recognise, but may need addressing. Please give me/ us your strength to carry on in this day and the following week.

Thank you, Lord. Amen

2) Think about this last week.

How have you got on with the activities this last week?

Note: If you set any goals and attempted or completed any. If you have or have not done anything different, say how and why. How did this make you feel? Any improvements?

_____
_____
_____
_____
_____
_____
_____
_____
_____
_____

_____

_____

_____

3) Think about your reactions to people and situations when they don't go to plan or irritate you. For each of the following, Check the most accurate box.

	Yes	Sometimes	No
Do you jump to conclusions often?			
Do you find it difficult to communicate?			
Do you focus on negative aspects?			
Do you believe the person/situation won't change?			
Do you find yourself accusing or being confrontational?			
Do you believe the person/situation isn't fair?			

Do you find yourself believing the other person/ situation should change to suit you?			

If you ticked 4+ in the 'yes' and 'occasionally' boxes, you may be experiencing frustration or anger, whether obvious to you or not, therefore, continue below. If less that 4 have a look first at the following questions, you may discover something new! Then prayerfully decide whether or not to skip to the following week, if working independently. Or if working in a group, support and encourage others.

Did you know?
Anger that is unexpressed and unprocessed can result in high levels of stress, which can damage an individual's mental and physical health.
(NSA, 2020)

---

4) Do you ever display physical aggression, sarcasm or passive-aggressive behaviours?
E.g. Resistance or a refusal to engage in activities with others, comments and speech.

_____
_____
_____
_____
_____
_____

_____
_____
_____
_____
_____
_____

Or if you do not express anger overtly, do you find yourself being cynical or carry out any form of self-harm?

_____
_____
_____
_____
_____
_____
_____
_____
_____
_____
_____
_____

Think about if you may be experiencing any underlying thoughts and ideas that maintain feelings of frustration or anger.

E.g., If you become inappropriately angry at every little injustice, this may indicate that you believe that the world 'should' be a fair place.

Then think about whether this belief is justified or not.

_____
_____
_____

_____
_____
_____
_____
_____
_____
_____
_____
_____

Are there specific situations, people, events that lead to feelings of frustration or anger?

Think about what the reasons may be as to why these lead to those feelings.

_____
_____
_____
_____
_____
_____
_____
_____
_____
_____
_____
_____

Anger can also be a reaction to underlying emotions. Have a think about what these could be.

E.g., sadness, grief, frustration, hurt, insecurity, threat.

_____
_____

_____
_____
_____
_____
_____
_____
_____
_____
_____
_____

5) Have a read through of the following techniques to help address anger management.

STOPP:
Stop, **T**ake a breath, **O**bserve, **P**ull back & **P**ractice.
This technique will need to be put to practice and repeated before it can become a habit.

Visualise:
Imagine a situation which may trigger feelings of anger. Then imagine yourself responding in a calm manner. When repeated enough it can help to deal with the situation if/when it arises.

Alternative Channelling:
Find alternative ways of channelling feelings of anger. E.g., Exercise, painting

Relaxation techniques:
Breathing exercises; Breathing in for 5 seconds then out for 5 seconds. Imagining your anger leaving your breath and calmness on the in breath.

Mindfulness; Refer to the section 'Mindfulness.'

Meditation; Refer to the section 'How to Practice Biblical Meditation.'

(NSA, 2020)

6) If you are working individually; read back through these and analyse what you have written, take in your responses and think about which techniques might be useful for you.

If you are in a group, discuss these, share and encourage each other.

7) Again, Pray...

- ♦ Thank Him for being present and helping you through this session.
- ♦ Offer to God your reactions, thoughts, feelings and behaviours.
- ♦ Ask Him to come to you and help you address these and any other underlying issues and emotions.
- ♦ Ask Him to guide you through these techniques and to help you overcome these issues.

This week:

- → Keep referring back to what you wrote today and remind yourself of the techniques, putting these into practice as often as possible.

→ Keep a diary, note down, feelings, behaviours and any triggers that you may come across. You can use the space below.

→ Practice biblical meditation, using the following scriptures and any that God puts on your heart.

Meditation

Follow the guide on page 29 'How to practice Biblical Meditation'.

Suggested scriptures:

Proverbs 15.4 The soothing tongue is a tree of life, but a perverse tongue crushes the spirit.

Psalm 37.7-8 Be still before the Lord and wait patiently for Him; do not fret when people succeed in their ways, when they carry out their wicked schemes. Refrain from anger and turn from wrath; do not fret- it leads only to evil.

Ephesians 4.31 Get rid of all bitterness, rage and anger, brawling and slander, along with every form of malice. Be kind and compassionate to one another, forgiving each other, just as Christ God gave you.

Lauren Roskilly

Thought Diary

Session Six:
Attitude and Gratitude

1) Firstly, let's pray...

Dear Lord,

Thank you for being with me/us today. Please be with me/us as I/we go through this session. Guide thoughts and feelings and draw to attention anything I/we don't yet recognise, but may need addressing. Please give me/ us your strength to carry on in this day and the following week.

Thank you, Lord. Amen

2) Think about this last week.

How have you got on with the activities for this last week?

Note: Did you try any of the techniques? How did you do this and why. How did it make you feel? Any improvements?

_____
_____
_____
_____
_____

_____
_____
_____
_____
_____
_____
_____

3) Answer the following questions.

Think about your attitude. Do you focus more on the positives or negatives in your life?

_____
_____
_____
_____
_____
_____
_____
_____
_____
_____
_____
_____

Do you find yourself believing the worst will happen or has happened? Or do you minimise the importance of any positives that occur?

_____
_____
_____

_____
_____
_____
_____
_____
_____
_____
_____
_____

Now think of instances where particular problems or situations have occurred. How do you view these? Do you feel consumed about the situation and unable to address any issues or do you think about how to go about improving or overcoming them?
If you normally feel consumed, think about ways in which you could improve or overcome a situation.

_____
_____
_____
_____
_____
_____
_____
_____
_____
_____
_____

If you encounter situations and circumstances that aren't at all possible to change, improve or overcome, then can you think of ways in which you can improve your situation or simply make it easier to manage?

E.g., A chronic illness; perhaps there are aids and adaptations to assist you. Or think about your capabilities and focus on them rather than any limitations. (This may not be easy, but by developing new, positive habits can improve your mental well-being.)

_____
_____
_____
_____
_____
_____
_____
_____
_____
_____
_____

4) Now think about right now, today, this week. Think about anything you could be thankful for? Write down everything you can think of.

E.g., A roof over your head, a friend, food.

_____
_____
_____
_____

_____
_____
_____
_____
_____
_____
_____

Did you know?
Gratitude is strongly and consistently associated with greater happiness. Gratitude helps people feel more positive emotions, relish good experiences, improve their health, deal with adversity, and build strong relationships.
(Harvard, 2020)

---

5) How about trying an experiment? Can you think of a new way of living that could improve your way of thinking? What could you do between now and the next session that would prove you were on the right track?

E.g., Keep notes each day for everything you are thankful for.

_____
_____
_____
_____
_____
_____
_____
_____

_____
_____
_____
_____

6) If you are working individually; Read back through these and analyse what you have written, take in your responses and think about the techniques. Practise how you might respond to certain situations.

If you are in a group, discuss these, share and encourage each other. Practice roleplaying in pairs; acting out potential issues/circumstances and focusing on your responses.

Practising these out loud can help the way you respond if or when a situation may occur.

7) Again, Pray...

- ♦ Thank God for anything positive in your life right now or in the world around you.
- ♦ Ask God to guide your thoughts and decisions, towards achieving your goals, according to His will.

This week:

- → Keep referring back to what you wrote today and remind yourself of what you are thankful for.

- → Keep a diary, note down, feelings, behaviours and any situations that you come across, note down how you respond to these. You can use the 'Thought Diary' space below.

→ Practice biblical meditation, using the following scriptures and any that God puts on your heart.

Meditation

Follow the guide on page 29 'How to practice Biblical Meditation'.

Suggested scriptures:

Romans 8.27 And he who searches hearts knows what is the mind of the Spirit, because the spirit intercedes for the saints according to the will of God.

Philippians 3.14 I press on toward the goal to win the prize for which God has called me heavenward in Christ Jesus.

Philippians 4.8 Whatever is true, whatever is noble, whatever is right, whatever is pure, whatever is lovely, whatever is admirable- if anything is excellent or praiseworthy- think about such things.

John 1.5 The light shines in the darkness, and the darkness has not overcome it.

Lauren Roskilly

Thought Diary

_____
_____
_____
_____
_____
_____
_____
_____
_____
_____
_____
_____
_____
_____
_____
_____
_____
_____
_____
_____
_____
_____
_____
_____
_____
_____
_____
_____
_____
_____
_____
_____
_____
_____
_____
_____
_____
_____
_____
_____

Session Seven:

Beliefs

1) Firstly, let's pray...

Dear Lord,

Thank you for being with me/us today. Please be with me/us as I/we go through this session. Guide thoughts and feelings and draw to attention anything I/we don't yet recognise, but may need addressing. Please give me/ us your strength to carry on in this day and the following week.

Thank you, Lord. Amen

2) Think about this last week.

How have you got on with the activities for the week?

Note: How did you get on thinking about what you are thankful for? If you have or have not done anything different and say how and why. How did this make you feel? Any improvements?

_____
_____
_____
_____
_____
_____
_____
_____

_____

_____

_____

_____

Did you know?
People who use the phrases "should", "must" and "ought to" tend to be harsh on themselves and expect too much from others. These phrases can be overused by individuals with maladaptive thinking styles.
(NSA, 2020)

---

3) Do you believe that you should or shouldn't say and do certain things or behave in certain ways? What are they?

E.g., As a parent/carer, do you believe you can't or shouldn't do anything certain things or for yourself?

_____

_____

_____

_____

_____

_____

_____

_____

_____

_____

_____

_____

Why do you believe you should or should not do or say certain things?

E.g., Worried about what others think.

_____

_____

_____

_____

_____

_____

_____

_____

_____

_____

_____

_____

What do you believe would happen if you did or didn't do those things?

Is that belief realistic? If so, would that affect you and your well - being or that of others?

_____

_____

_____

_____

_____

_____

_____

_____

_____

_____

_____

_____

Do you believe that everything you do impacts other people or external events? Do you believe that you are to blame for the negative things happening around you? Why?

_____
_____
_____
_____
_____
_____
_____
_____
_____
_____
_____
_____

Are these thoughts the truth? What would you say to someone you love who believes these things? Would you honestly agree with them? Why or why not?

_____
_____
_____
_____
_____
_____
_____
_____
_____
_____
_____

4) Now think about the above situations. Imagine you did something you believed you should or shouldn't have done and then play in your mind, how the situation would unravel, thinking of the worst-case scenario. What happened? Was it as bad as you initially expected? Is there anything you could do or say to change the end result, if needed?

_____
_____
_____
_____
_____
_____
_____
_____
_____
_____
_____
_____

5) If you are working individually; read back through these and analyse what you have written, take in your responses and think about the techniques. Practise playing in your mind certain scenarios and how they end.

If you are in a group, discuss these, share and encourage each other. Practice roleplaying in pairs; acting out what you believe you should or should not do, do this several times and change the ending, including your response.

Imagining or practising these will help you realise the end results and the effects they have on yourself and others.

6) Again, Pray...

- Offer any "should" or "shouldn't" beliefs and your behaviours you have to God
- Ask Him to reveal any other distortive thoughts or behaviours you may have
- Thank Him for yourself and ask Him to help you think the way Jesus does.

This week:

→ Keep referring back to what you wrote today and remind yourself of His truths and those you learnt today.

→ Keep a diary, note down, feelings, behaviours and any situations that you come across, note down how you respond to these. You can use the 'Thought Diary' space below.

→ Practice biblical meditation, using the following scriptures and any that God puts on your heart.

Meditation

Follow the guide on page 29 'How to practice Biblical Meditation'.

Suggested scriptures:

Romans 8:31 What, then, shall we say in response to these things? If God is for us, who can be against us?

2 Corinthians 10.5 We demolish arguments and every pretension that sets itself up against the knowledge of God, and we take captive every thought to make it obedient to Christ.

Proverbs 3.5-6 Trust in the Lord with all your heart, and do not lean on your own understanding. In all your ways acknowledge Him, and He will make straight your paths.

Lauren Roskilly

Thought Diary

_____
_____
_____
_____
_____
_____
_____
_____
_____
_____
_____
_____
_____
_____
_____
_____
_____
_____
_____
_____
_____
_____
_____
_____
_____
_____
_____
_____
_____
_____

Session Eight:

Reassessment and Maintenance

1) Firstly, let's pray...

Dear Lord,

Thank you for being with me/us today. Please be with me/us as I/we go through this session. Guide thoughts and feelings and draw to attention anything I/we don't yet recognise, but may need addressing. Please give me/ us your strength to carry on in this day and the following week.

Thank you, Lord. Amen

2) Think about this last week.

How have you got on with the activities for the week?

Note: Have you noticed any "should thoughts'" and overcome these with truths? If you have or have not done anything different and say how and why. How did this make you feel? Any improvements?

_____
_____
_____
_____
_____
_____
_____
_____

_____

_____

_____

_____

3) For this final session we will revisit the checklist from the first session.

So, looking at the following list, check the box next to the symptoms you have experienced in the past two weeks.

Psychological Symptoms

Feelings of sadness	
A loss of interest in activities	
Low self-esteem	
Feelings of guilt	
A tendency to cry or feeling on the edge of tears	
Irritability and intolerance	
Little or no motivation	
Difficulty in making decisions	
Feelings of anxiety or worry	
Self-harm or thoughts of self-harm	
Suicide attempts or thoughts of suicide	

Physical symptoms

Moving or speaking more slowly than usual	
Changes in weight or appetite	
Constipation	
Aches and pains that have no obvious explanation	
Low energy levels	
Loss of libido	
Changes to menstrual cycle (in women)	
Disturbed sleep (trouble staying asleep, waking up too early or sleeping too much)	

Compare your result with that from the first session. Hopefully you have noticed an improvement.

If you have ticked above 5: Revisit each or specific sessions again.

If you have ticked above 10: Make arrangements to speak with your G.P, speak to someone from your church in leadership and revisit each session.

(These sessions can be completed as often as necessary.)

4) What stress, circumstances and problems are you experiencing in your life right now?

_____

_____

_____

_____

_____
_____
_____
_____
_____
_____
_____
_____

Do these affect your thoughts, feelings, behaviour and mood?

_____
_____
_____
_____
_____
_____
_____
_____
_____
_____
_____
_____

Compare these responses to those you made in session three. Have they improved since then? Answer yes or no and explain why you think this may be.

_____
_____
_____
_____
_____

_____
_____
_____
_____
_____
_____
_____

5) In order to maintain healthy thought processes there are a few things to keep in mind:

❖ Recognising Triggers: Think about what might trigger any negative or unhelpful thoughts, feelings or behaviours. E.g., situations, people, places. Then, by recognising these, it can improve your ability of how you respond to these.

❖ Journal: Keeping a note and working through your thoughts and feelings. This doesn't have to be every time they arise but if you make journaling a habit, once a day or a few times a week, it can help to release these feelings as opposed to pushing them down and ignoring them. Then give these thoughts and feelings to God; asking Him to take them away and fill you with His Holy Spirit instead.

❖ Routine: Include self-care and activities you enjoy, within your daily routine. By doing this you will boost serotonin levels which will, in turn, boost your mood. Include reading scripture, prayer and biblical meditation into this routine as well.

Use the space below to make some notes on these.

_____
_____
_____
_____
_____
_____
_____
_____
_____
_____
_____
_____

6) If you are working individually, reflect through this week's notes and think about any areas you may want to revisit, if any. If not, think of the progress you have made and reward yourself by doing something from your activities you enjoy list.

If you are working as a group, reflect through this week's notes, think about if you would like to revisit any, or not and share with each other. Making sure to praise and encourage each other.

7) Again, Pray...

- Offer God everything from this session
- Thank God for His guidance throughout
- Ask Him to help you in the next chapter of your journey and to remind you of what you have learnt and that you can do all things

through Him who strengthens you. *(Philippians 4.13)*

This week and beyond:

Practice what you have learnt these past eight weeks. The more something is practiced, the easier it becomes. Then, in turn, it can be part of you and your life.

Revisit any time you like, for reference or to go through again. Use the scriptures for meditation and the techniques provided.

Keep your focus on God and He will guide your path.

<u>**Meditation**</u>

Follow the guide on page 29 'How to practice Biblical Meditation'.

Suggested scriptures:

Psalms 23.3 He refreshes my soul. He guides me along the right paths for his names sake.

Psalm 73.24 You guide me with your counsel, and afterward you will take me into glory.

Psalm 31.3 Since you are my rock and my fortress, for the sake of your name lead and guide me.

Testimonies

These testimonies are from people offering their story on how God has helped them in their lives and with their mental health. Please note the stars * for trigger warning level.

Richard H H Johnston *

I experienced depression for the first time over 20 years ago. I got fired from a job I loved for no good reason (I suppose I got in the way of other people's ambition and asked too many awkward questions). I remember looking across the room at someone I expected to exercise a measured approach with kindness. "That's it," he said. "You're terminated". It's what I now describe as my Arnold Schwarzenegger moment. From a board room meeting I had to walk along the corridor, clear my desk and hand back the keys for the office I had set up from scratch. I was escorted off the premises and walked out into the cold, fresh air. For me it was a devastating trauma that sent shock waves through my whole world.

One of my best friends was instrumental in the process of getting me fired. He never spoke to me about what happened. Never provided any explanation to me as a friend. Never contacted me to ask how I was. It was as if I didn't exist. Over that period, I also experienced death threats.

I went into hiding for several months. I was so low that

I went back and forth from bed to couch for months, rarely venturing out to the shops. Daytime turned into night-time and I slept at least 12-16 hours every day for weeks. I could hardly drag myself out of bed. The weight of grief was so heavy that I felt crushed. A few Christian friends and family members supported me over that period. But I hardly read my Bible or prayed at all. I didn't know what to pray or say to God. The best prayer I had was "Oh God please help! I don't understand!"

It felt like all of the spiritual lights had been turned off, the door to God seemed locked shut and maybe the key had been thrown away.

It was out of that very dark place that I gradually began to experience healing and restoration. In my weakness and brokenness, I knew that God was the strength of my heart. He had shown me treasures out of darkness and abundant grace, mercy and tender-ness for each new day. I'm so thankful for what God has done in my life but I still have bad days. Days when the dark clouds roll in and everything seems shrouded in a deep dank fog. But the darkness has taught me something strange and unexpected.

I will give you the treasures of darkness and the riches hidden in secret places, so that you may know that I am the LORD, the God of Israel, who calls you by name (Isaiah 45:3)

He has written a new story into my life and I have experienced beauty for ashes and a garment of praise instead of a spirit of despair.

Catherine Cooley *

Two years ago, in 2017, I was pregnant with my Daughter Aeryn (Erin) when I was hit by a drunk driver who was driving a moving truck. While I survived the crash, my daughter did not. Afterwards, my emotional and mental health crashed. I began plotting suicide. I created two plans each time being prevented by my husband. I started to see a therapist and was diagnosed with depression, generalized anxiety, and PTSD. Moving forward was hard. I was too angry and heartbroken and was angry at God. I tried forcing myself to do those, but I never achieved them.

I struggled with the "why." Why did He let this happen? Why me? I stopped praying and reading scripture.

Then God gave me a "who do you think you are" moment.

The best way I can describe it was very much like a father correcting a child. At that moment everything hit me. Yes, I was hurting and I was angry at the Creator of everything. I was being hateful towards the Lord who loves me with unmeasurable depths. But I realised that even though I was in so much pain, I was being sinful. I repented and started a long journey of moving forward. This helped me scratch the surface of how much God loves me. If I could've walked away, I would have. I was that angry at Him. But no matter how hard I pushed away God just pulled me closer to Him. It was truly a parenting moment in which he had to correct my heart in order to help me heal in a healthy, positive way with Him at the centre.

Anna Redman **

I had a good upbringing, despite my parents divorcing when I was a toddler. My father had no contact with us, as he was an alcoholic. He died when I was a teenager and as I never knew him, I didn't go to his funeral.

We moved to the west country when I was eleven and something in me changed. I began to feel that I didn't fit in anywhere. I thought I was ugly, awkward and stupid. With hindsight, the enemy had a field day with me. I started rebelling at about fourteen; smoking, drinking and bunking off school. Somehow, I managed to scrape through my GCSEs and went on to college. I did really well in higher education and became a qualified PA, passed my driving test and went on to work. When I left home, I worked but partied hard at the weekend.

I was quite promiscuous and got pregnant at 18. It was a total shock and I decided to have an abortion. At the time, I really believed that the baby growing inside of me was just a "clump of cells". My heart is breaking as I write this, as I know this is a lie from the pit of hell. I never fell pregnant again, as I later found out that I had blocked fallopian tubes - a consequence of my promiscuity.

At twenty-one, I got engaged. Even though I was living in sin, I never touched drugs. Not out of principal but because they were just never in my social circle. My fiancé turned out to be a heroin addict and I started dabbling. I quickly became hooked and life spiralled downhill then. Over the next couple of years, I lost my job, lost my driving license, got arrested, stole from my family, overdosed regularly, started injecting rather than smoking. I became a junkie.

I went into a secular rehab in my mid-twenties and managed to stay clean for the duration of the programme. However, without God in my life, I soon returned to using. I tried rehab again ten years later, I received two prison sentences, lived with a drug dealer and started prostituting. Another ten years later and several attempts of getting clean through NA meetings, I realised that I could not beat addiction on my own strength. I had no fight left and attempted suicide. I landed in three different psychiatric units. It was when I was at the end of myself that God stepped in. I was visited in the Psychiatric Unit by a Christian that I had met through NA and he led me through the prayer of salvation. Upon my release, I joined a Church and got baptised. I was still quite unwell, so they sent me to Teen Challenge where I received excellent discipleship. I gave up smoking and came off the antidepressants, as I was depressed because of what I'd become.

I was so broken and hostile, but the staff treated me with mercy and grace (as well as discipline when necessary!) I left in November 2017 and got plugged into a Church where I do services with the youth. I gained qualifications and got a paid job in a Night Shelter.

My outlook upon life has now changed drastically. I used to be negative, afraid, critical, resentful and full of guilt and shame. Now, I am hopeful and much more compassionate, happy, patient and peaceful. My relationships with other people have improved beyond measure, as my walls are coming down bit by bit. God is so gentle in His loving-kindness and has never given me more than I can handle. I am learning to rest and abide in God's love, rather than striving all the time.

Elaine Curry *

I grew up in a Christian family but when I was fourteen, I watched a video on Revelation that totally filled me with fear and horror.

The message of Jesus was very confusing to me during church services and I made up my mind that church wasn't for me. I grew up with the perception that you had to be so pure and sinless to be a Christian and that I couldn't live up to the strict standards of Christians. I had two Christian brothers. One of my brothers that I looked up to very much lost his faith. I was sad to see him slip away and lose his faith in God.

I battled the good and bad voices in my head for many years, where many temptations and weakness-es appeared.

Later, I found myself a victim to domestic violence which ended in a separation.

Work gave me focus during tough emotional days and my financial stability for my daughter and I to be independent without abuse.

I lived with high anxiety, fear, disappointment and dips of depression in my twenties and thirties in very unhealthy relationships always hoping to find love.

I then became curious about the Spirit world; The New Age, Law of attraction, Angel cards, Astrology, Love activation cards etc.

When I hit 40 I cried and asked God to help me. Although the Gospel was far from my mind, I was in a spiritual battle finding the truth.

I went to a 'Food for the Soul' event in Spring of 2017. There was a group of people sitting and they had a stand that said 'Free Prayers' with the Holy Spirit. They saw me and asked me if I want prayer but I said that Christianity wasn't for me and that I had been so hurt by Christians in the past.

They said they were sorry to hear that and I let them pray for me. As they started to pray, I was moved to tears and shaking with trapped emotions – it was the most beautiful prayer and I felt the presence of the Holy Spirit for the first time – it was real.

A week later I was out with my friend Donna and I got so drunk I was physically sick. But that night I knew something different was inside me and I was more aware of my actions. I went straight home and cried myself to sleep. I got up the next day and cried out to the Lord to help me. After this my conversations with God started.

Two weeks later a man called Amine came into my life, a very spiritual man. I was spiritually awoken and meeting someone to have conversations about God with was very refreshing.

I disappeared from the social scene to spend time getting to know God, explore faith and find my purpose of being. Amine led me onto the right path to restore my obedience and faith in God. But in the first year of Christianity, I cried and sobbed more – I actually thought something was wrong with me but I was mourning my old life. During this rebirthing and an empty nest, with my daughter flying away, my anxiety increased, panic attacks got worse and I was going through a spiritual awakening. I was reading the bible - prioritising changing my new way of life and seeing the world through different eyes. I found the importance of the word of God, the presence of my comforter and the Holy Spirit. My repenting and acceptance of Jesus as my saviour saw a renewal of my spirit - there was a conversion, a change of mind and behaviours. I began to feel different, act different, talk to people differently and see things differently and through God's eyes. I finally felt I had plugged into the meaning of life with a powerful love that was beyond my own explanations.

Dawn Shailer

Cross Rhythms radio was a big help for me when I lived in the town where it was broadcast from - so very loud and clear!
I was diagnosed with thyroid cancer and felt very scared and lonely, but the staff at the radio and I forged relationships that would lead me to becoming Christian and harnessing prayer like never I never had before.
I'm so glad I got in contact with them!
My very first album that I ordered was called 'Return of the Overcomers' from a Christian film track and also listened to powerful music from Music of Black Origin as I needed something dynamic and strong.
Rydels 'the fight' and 'we shall overcome' played many times and I still fall back on those tracks now.
I adore worship and praise Jesus for his effect in my life now and forever.

Bibliography

APS (2012) *Remembering the Father of Cognitive Psychology* in 'Association for Psychological Science' (Online) Available at: https://www.psychologicalscience.org/observer/remembering-the-father-of-cognitive-psychology Accessed on 11/11/2020

Burton, Neel, M.D. (2020) *10 Simple Ways To Improve Your Mood When Your Feeling Down* in 'Psychology Today' (Online) Available at: https://www.psychologytoday.com/gb/blog/hide-and-seek/201701/10-simple-ways-improve-your-mood-when-youre-feeling-down Accessed on 14/11/2020

Cloud, H. and Townsend, J. (2017) *Boundaries* Dr Henry Cloud and Dr John Townsend, Zondervan, Harper Collins Publishing, USA

Emerald Works (2022) *SMART Goals* in 'Mind Tools' (Online)Available at: https://www.mindtools.com/pages/article/smart-goals.htm Accessed on: 17/11/2020

Harvard (2020) *Giving thanks can make you happier* in 'Harvard Health Publishing, Harvard Medical School' (Online) Available at: https://www.health.harvard.edu/healthbeat/giving-thanks-can-make-you-happier Accessed on: 17/11/2020

NHS (2019) *Symptoms- Psychosis* in 'NHS' (Online) Available at:

https://www.nhs.uk/conditions/psychosis/symptoms/ Accessed on 09/11/2020

NSA (2020) *Module 1: The Underlying Principles Behind CBT* in 'Cognitive Behavioural Therapy (CBT) Diploma' (Online) Available at: https://newskillsacademy.co.uk/lesson/module-1-underlying-principles-behind-cbt/ Accessed 11/11/2020

NSA (2020) *Module 4: Case Formulation, Irrational Beliefs & The ABC Model* in 'Cognitive Behavioural Therapy (CBT) Diploma' (Online) Available at: https://newskillsacademy.co.uk/lesson/module-4-case-formulation-irrational-beliefs-abc-model/ Accessed 06/11/2020

NSA (2020) *Module 5: Planning a CBT session* in 'Cognitive Behavioural Therapy (CBT) Diploma' (Online) Available at: https://newskillsacademy.co.uk/lesson/module-5-planning-cbt-session/ Accessed 06/11/2020

NSA (2020) *Module 7: Further CBT Techniques* in 'Cognitive Behavioural Therapy (CBT) Diploma' (Online) Available at: https://newskillsacademy.co.uk/lesson/module-7-cbt-techniques/ Accessed 06/11/2020

NSA (2020) *Module 9: Using CBT in the treatment of Excessive Anger and Insomnia* in 'Cognitive Behavioural Therapy (CBT) Diploma' (Online) Available at https://newskillsacademy.co.uk/lesson/module-9-using-cbt-treatment-excessive-anger-insomnia-2/ Accessed 13/11/2020

Lauren Roskilly

SMHC (2019) *5 Tips for setting goals* in 'Serenity Mental Health Centres' (Online) Available at: https://serenitymentalhealthcenters.com/5-tips-for-setting-and-keeping-mental-health-goals/ Accessed on 14/11/2020

The Open University (2009) 'Mental Health Still Matters,' Palgrave Macmillan (2009) The Open University, Walton Hall, Milton Keynes, United Kingdom

The Open University (2014) 'Mental Health,' The Open University, Walton Hall, Milton Keynes, United Kingdom

The Open University (2015) 'Mental Health and Community', The Open University, Walton Hall, Milton Keynes, United Kingdom

Unberson, D. and Montez, J. (2011) *Social Relationships and Health: A Flashpoint for Health Policy* In 'The National Center for Biotechnology Information' (Online) Available at: The National Center for Biotechnology Information Accessed 13/01/2021

WHO (2020) *Mental Health* in 'Word Health Organisation' (Online) Available at: https://www.who.int/mental_health/who_urges_investment/en/#:~:text=WHO%2FP.,to%20her%20or%20his%20community. Accessed 23/11/2020

Index

Habit- 44, 69, 77, 84, 101
Holy Spirit- 27-9, 101, 33, 35

Illness- 33, 84

Journal- 38, 101

Leadership- 39, 42, 99

Maintenance- 97-103
Medicine- 21
Meditation- 29, 37, 39, 42, 46, 52, 54, 62, 69, 70, 77, 79, 87, 94-5, 101, 103
Mindfulness- 26-9, 77
Mood- 57-8, 64, 100, 101

Neisser, Ulrich- 23
NHS- 25

PAPAS ART- 65
Peace- 27-8, 64
Perception-23, 34
Phobias-67
Physical- 19-21, 41, 74, 99
Prayer- 28-9, 33, 37-8, 40, 45, 48, 52-3, 56, 61, 64, 68, 72, 74, 78, 81, 86, 89, 94, 97, 101-2
Psychosis- 21

Relationship- 56-61, 66, 85
Relax- 42, 44, 77
Relaxation Techniques- 77
Resilience- 19, 24, 37
Responses- 19, 37-8, 48-54, 61, 68, 78, 86, 94
Routine-69, 101

About the Author

Lauren has been on her Christian walk since 2005. She is a mum of two beautiful children and has a BA Hons in Health and Social Care, a diploma in CBT and an Accredited Life Coach certification.

She is transparent about her past ups and downs with mental health, depression, anxiety and self- harm. But she has learnt to refocus from unhealthy and negative mindsets and towards Christ. Thus, the name of her ministry, 'Mindful of Christ'. She is also the author of 'Indestructible Faith- prayers & prompts for journaling' and co-author of the #1 Bestseller 'Worship in the Wilderness: Let Praise Lead the Way.'

As a Speaker and Christian Life Coach she helps people to recognise & overcome unhealthy and negative mindsets and helps them to discover and step into their identity and God given purpose. She has previously spoken on podcasts, radio and TV.

Lauren is also available for:
- Coaching
- Speaking Events (in- person & online)
- Writing; guest blog posts, devotionals, freelance writing, bible studies etc.

Website: www.mindfulofchrist.net
Social Media: @Mindful of Christ
YouTube | LinkedIn | Instagram | Facebook | Twitter

Printed in Great Britain
by Amazon